HISTORY'S MYSTERIES

REAL-LIFE MONSTERS?

By Therese Shea

Gareth Stevens
PUBLISHING

Please visit our website, www.garethstevens.com. For a free color catalog of all our high-quality books, call toll free 1-800-542-2595 or fax 1-877-542-2596.

Library of Congress Cataloging-in-Publication Data

Shea, Therese.
Real-life monsters? / by Therese Shea.
p. cm. — (History's mysteries)
Includes index.
ISBN 978-1-4824-2094-4 (pbk.)
ISBN 978-1-4824-2093-7 (6-pack)
ISBN 978-1-4824-2095-1 (library binding)
1. Monsters — Juvenile literature. 2. Animals, Mythical —Juvenile literature. I. Shea, Therese. II. Title.
GR825.S54 2015
398—d23

First Edition

Published in 2015 by
Gareth Stevens Publishing
111 East 14th Street, Suite 349
New York, NY 10003

Designer: Katelyn E. Reynolds
Editor: Therese Shea

Photo credits: Cover, p. 1 Nomad_Soul/Shutterstock.com; cover, pp. 1–32 (background texture) Randi Scott/Shutterstock.com; p. 5 Sparkling Moments Photography/Shutterstock.com; p. 7 (Bigfoot) Grambo Grambo/First Light/Getty Images; p. 7 (map) Fiziker/Wikipedia.com; pp. 9, 22 Popperfoto/Getty Images; p. 11 Federico Rostagno/Shutterstock.com; p. 12 Christina Gascoigne/Robert Harding World Imagery/Getty Images; p. 13 Michael Zysman/Shutterstock.com; p. 14 Margaret M Stewart/Shutterstock.com; p. 15 salajean/Shutterstock.com; p. 17 Imagno/Hulton Archive/Getty Images; p. 18 TsuneoMP/Shutterstock.com; p. 19 The British Library/Robana/Getty Images; p. 20 Victor Habbick/Shutterstock.com; p. 21 Jeff J Mitchell/Getty Images; p. 23 Keystone/Hulton Archive/Getty Images; p. 25 (megalodon) Ethan Miller/Getty Images; p. 25 (*Spinosaurus*) Junko Kimura/Getty Images; p. 27 (mosquito) Anest/Shutterstock.com; p. 27 (crocodile) Richard Grande/AFP/Getty Images; p. 28 Mgiganteus1/Wikipedia.com; p. 29 (green anacondo) Alberto Loyo/Shutterstock.com; p. 29 (tarantula) Ivan Smuk/Shutterstock.com; p. 29 (vampire bat) Eduard Kyslynskyy/Shutterstock.com.

Printed in the United States of America

CPSIA compliance information: Batch #CW15GS: For further information contact Gareth Stevens, New York, New York at 1-800-542-2595.

CONTENTS

Words in the glossary appear in **bold** type the first time they are used in the text.

A REAL-LIFE MONSTER?

When you hear a bump, crash, or thud in the middle of the night, do you think it's your parents making noise? Or maybe it's your dog? Perhaps your imagination really takes over, and you picture some sort of monster! It's easy to get scared in the dark at night. But do you really have to be frightened of monsters in real life? It depends what you call a monster.

In this book, we'll investigate some scary creatures. While some probably exist only in the pages of books and in the movies, others were actual creatures that are now extinct. And for some of these monsters, people can't decide if they're real or not! You can choose for yourself what you believe about these things. Whether they're real-life monsters or not, they're fascinating to learn about.

REVEALED!

The word "monster" comes from the Latin word *monere*, which means "to warn."

WHAT'S A MONSTER?

There are several definitions of "monster" in the dictionary. One is "a strange and horrible imaginary creature." Another is "an animal of strange or scary shape." Yet another says a monster is "something extremely large." From these definitions, you can understand why a blue whale, the largest animal on Earth, could be described as a monster—because of its size. But a vampire or a tarantula could also be called a monster for its terrifying features!

Our eyes seem to play tricks on us at night. We may see a shadow and think it's something else.

BIGFOOT

Once in a while, a news story pops up about Bigfoot. A hiker or camper may claim to have seen one in a dark, dense forest somewhere. Usually, that's followed by more sightings and yet more accounts about people's experiences with these strange creatures. That's right—"creatures." "Bigfoot" is the name given to any large, hairy, humanlike creature that walks on two legs. People who believe in them think they hide in the forests of North America, especially the Pacific Northwest.

Most reports of Bigfoots note that the creatures are much larger than the average person and have a rotten smell. Usually, Bigfoots run away when they're sighted. However, occasionally, angry Bigfoots are said to throw rocks at people or try to break into cabins!

REVEALED!

Another name for Bigfoot is Sasquatch.

EVIDENCE?

Some people say they have evidence of Bigfoot other than their own eyes. They claim they have taken photos of the creature. A few even have video. Other people have found only tracks of the creatures left in snow and mud. That's enough to convince them. However, people who don't believe in Bigfoots think this evidence is fake. They say that blurry photos and videos are just people dressed up. Footprints can be faked, too. What do you believe?

BIGFOOT SIGHTINGS IN NORTH AMERICA

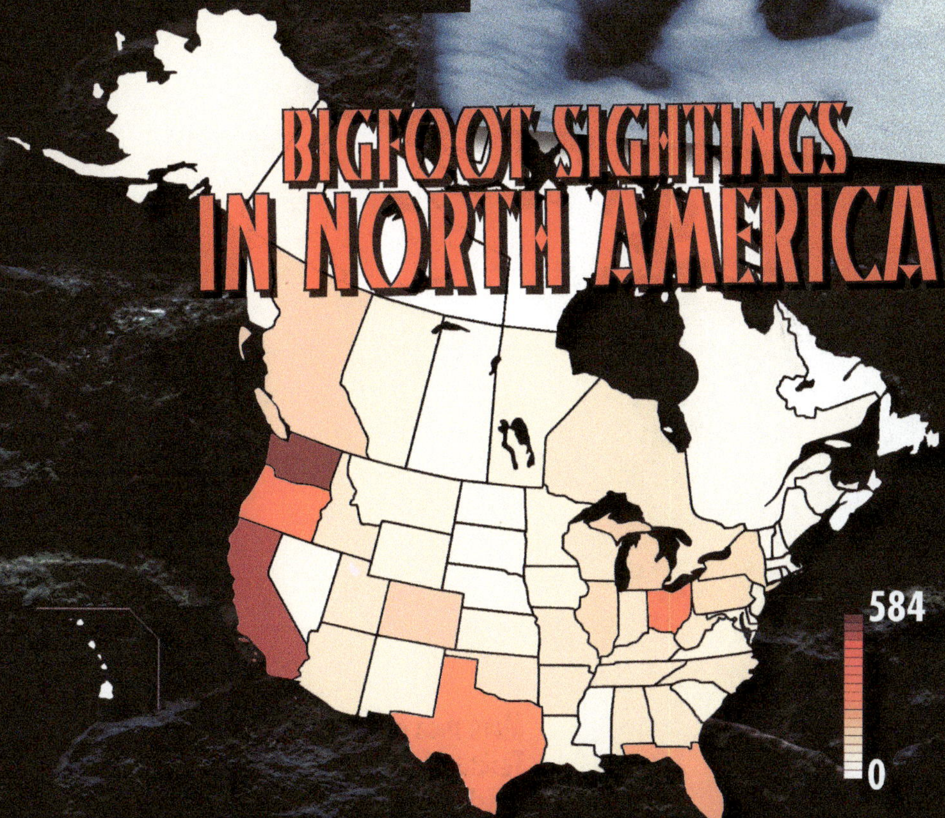

According to the Bigfoot Field Researchers Organization, Washington State has had the most Bigfoot sightings with 584. California is close behind with 427 sightings.

YETI

The Yeti is a monster (or monsters) said to live in the snow-covered Himalaya mountain range of Asia. Like Bigfoot, people say it walks on two feet, but this humanlike creature has white hair or fur all over its body that helps it blend in with snow. Sightings of the Yeti are more rare than sightings of Bigfoot. However, one mountain climber claimed to have come within 30 feet (9 m) of a Yeti in 1986. Many more explorers have reported seeing markings in the snow that could have been made by such a creature.

Scientists have found white hair in caves in the Himalayas. In 2013, a sample of such hair was tested and found to match a kind of polar bear that lived more than 40,000 years ago. It was thought that these animals and their descendants died out a long time ago. Could they still exist and be mistaken for Yeti?

REVEALED!

More than a dozen people in the village of Tashtagol, Russia, said they have seen Yeti. A Russian scientist thinks these Yeti are relatives of Neanderthals, a type of early human.

BEAR OR YETI?

Some people think the footprints found in the Himalayan snow aren't made by Yeti but bears. Bears walk on all fours, and some place their back foot partly over their front foot's footprint. This makes a print that looks like a very large human footprint but pointing in the opposite direction than the bear is walking. Strange prints are also created by falling lumps of snow and rocks. Unfortunately, footprints are often quickly covered by a layer of snow, so they can't be tracked.

In 1951, a mountain climber took a picture of what he thought was a Yeti footprint. Yeti are also called **Abominable** Snowmen.

MUMMIES

Unlike Bigfoot and Yeti, we know mummies exist. We can see them in museums around the world today. Mummification, or the preservation of a dead body, can happen because of conditions in nature or through the actions of people. The ancient Egyptians are famous for their mummification process.

Although the Egyptian method of mummification changed throughout the years, the Egyptians always took out most of the body's organs, treated the body with salts to remove moisture, and wrapped the body in linen and cloth. The process could take as long as 70 days. All this was meant to make the body last because it was thought to be needed in the **afterlife**. This is also why the possessions of Egyptians were buried with them.

REVEALED!

In Egypt, the brain of the dead was removed from the skull with a long, thin hook!

WHO WERE MUMMIES?

Egyptians began mummifying people around 2600 BC. Usually, only wealthy or important ancient Egyptians were mummified, such as the Egyptian rulers called pharaohs. Only these few had the riches needed to pay for this long process as well as the tombs in which they were placed. Some people requested that their servants and even their pets be made mummies! Most common Egyptians, however, were buried in the sand. Dry, hot sand can also preserve bodies, though not as well.

Egyptians usually left the heart in the body throughout mummification, believing it to be the center of a person's being.

The Chinchorro people of Chile were practicing mummification 2,000 years before the Egyptians! They took bodies apart, reattached them using sticks and plant matter, and covered them in mud. This may have been a way to honor their dead.

Mummies have also been found high in the mountains of Peru. The Inca people used the cold, dry air there to mummify the dead. Mummified Inca children are thought to be offerings to the gods.

Human bodies have also been preserved in **peat bogs**. Peat bogs lack oxygen, an element that helps break down dead bodies. They do contain tannins, which are natural chemicals that can be used to turn animal skins into leather. These make "bog people" remarkably well preserved—and creepy!

REVEALED!

Some bog bodies have been found with a cut throat, broken bones, a rope around their neck, or other marks that suggest they were killed or murdered.

The Tollund Man, shown here, was found in a peat bog in Denmark with a rope around his neck. He lived in the fourth century BC.

CREEPY CURSES!

Mummies definitely look scary, but could they be called real-life monsters? You might think so if you believe in mummies' curses. When the tomb of Egyptian pharaoh Tutankhamun was discovered in 1922, some people spread the rumor that there was a curse written in the tomb. They said the curse doomed those who disturbed the tomb, especially after several of those people died. While this wasn't true of Tutankhamun's tomb, there were curses found in other tombs!

Chauchilla Cemetery in Peru contains mummified human remains such as this. The body was clothed in cotton, painted with a matter called resin, and kept in a tomb made from mud bricks.

VAMPIRES

Stories of vampires can be traced back to ancient Greece. There are many legends from many cultures that have been passed down for centuries about vampire-like creatures. Most stories focus on vampires as people who have died, but rise each night from their grave to suck blood with sharp fangs. Depending on the tale, the "undead" creature may be beautiful or ugly.

How does one become a vampire? Many tales say they turn after becoming bitten by another vampire. However, others say that magic can create a vampire—or even a cat jumping over a dead body! Methods of killing a vampire include plunging a spike through its heart, setting it on fire, and cutting off its head.

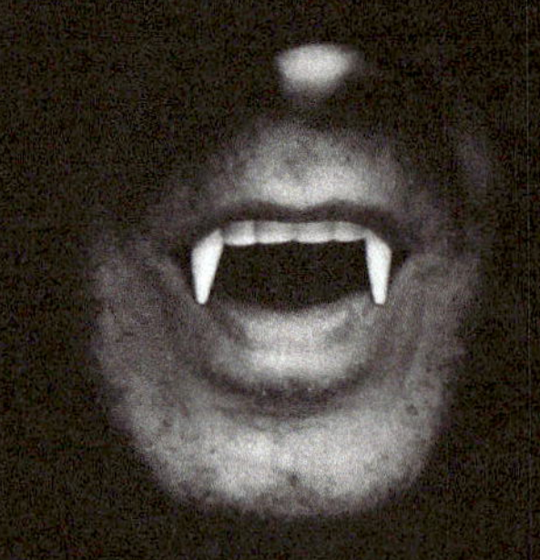

REVEALED!

Some legends say vampires have no reflection in a mirror and cannot be photographed.

STRIGOI

In Transylvania in Romania, vampires are called *strigoi*. At first, *strigoi* are the newly dead's invisible spirits who play tricks on the living. However, they later turn into visible creatures who walk the earth hoping to drink a person's blood right from their heart! To stop this from happening, people sometimes dug up the dead who were thought to be *strigoi* and either burned the body or put a spike through it.

Graves have been found with skeletons inside that were likely thought to be vampires. The heads have been removed from the bodies!

Vlad Dracula lived in Transylvania in the 1400s. Vlad, a prince, was known for being extremely cruel to his enemies. He's said to have impaled them, which means hanging their bodies on stakes. Centuries later, author Bram Stoker wrote a story about a vampire named Dracula who lived in Transylvania. Many vampires of fiction followed, often borrowing from Stoker.

However, throughout history, there have been those who believed in—and feared—vampires. In New England and Eastern Europe in the 1700s and 1800s, some speared the dead, hoping to prevent them from becoming vampires. Even in the early 2000s, Africans in Malawi claimed vampires were taking blood from them at night. Though the "vampires" used **syringes**, the people claimed they disappeared in front of their eyes!

VAMPIRES AND DISEASE

People particularly believed in vampires in times of disease. Before there was knowledge of disease, people blamed vampirism. For example, someone would fall ill with a disease, often **tuberculosis**. If that person died and the disease spread, it was thought to be the fault of the now "undead" victim, rising from the grave to kill more people. The disease itself wasn't blamed as people didn't understand how it spread.

REVEALED!

Families dug up their loved ones to burn their remains to stop the spread of sickness. If the dead person didn't look like their body was rotting, it was thought to be a sign they were really a vampire.

This portrait of Vlad Dracula is believed to be a true likeness of what the savage prince looked like.

WEREWOLVES

Werewolves populate storybooks almost as much as vampires. In **lore**, werewolves are people who turn into wolves at night. They change back into humans as the sun rises. In some stories, werewolves only transform—whether they want to or not—during a full moon. Once a werewolf, the savage beast roams to satisfy its hunger. It preys upon animals and people, alive and dead.

In the 1500s, belief in werewolves was widespread. Some people were even convicted and executed for being werewolves! In certain cases, the accused believed they really were werewolves. They might have even looked like werewolves. There's a medical condition called hypertrichosis that causes people to grow thick hair all over their body. **Rabies** and drug use may have also spread werewolf panic.

REVEALED!

The **psychiatric** condition in which a person believes they're a wolf is called lycanthropy.

WERE-ANIMALS WORLDWIDE

Although most werewolf lore seems to come from Europe, werewolf tales have been told around the world. The first mention of a man being turned into a wolf is in the *Epic of Gilgamesh*, a **Mesopotamian** poem from about 1800 BC. In places where wolves don't roam commonly, similar lore features other animals, such as werebears in Russia and weretigers in China. In the 1930s, researchers in Ghana reported a belief that people could turn into hyenas.

In some stories, werewolves don't remember what they've done once they've turned back into people.

THE LOCH NESS MONSTER

Every so often, there's a sighting of a large, long-necked creature in the waters of northern Scotland. And once again, many people begin musing about the possible existence of the Loch Ness Monster.

Far from being a new creation in the public's imagination, the first report of monsters in Loch Ness dates back to the seventh century. Scottish lore tells of beasts called water-kelpies who invited children to ride on their back. The children became stuck to the creatures and disappeared into the water forever.

Around 1933, a road was laid along Loch Ness. That year, a couple driving by reported seeing a large creature swimming along the water's surface. A local paper called the mystery animal the "Loch Ness Monster."

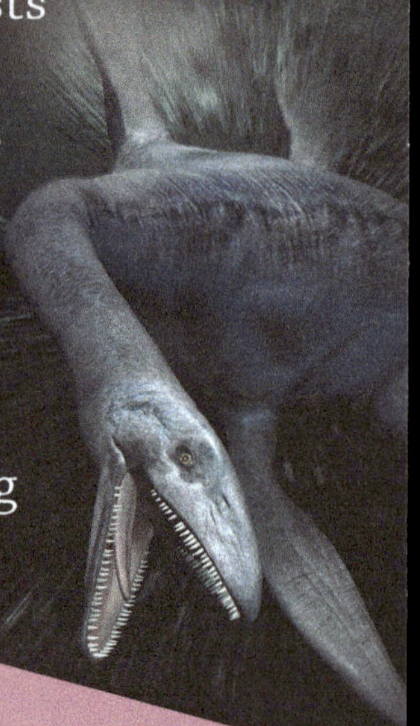

REVEALED!

In the first century AD, people who lived in northern Scotland carved pictures of a creature with a long neck and flippers. Could it have been the Loch Ness Monster?

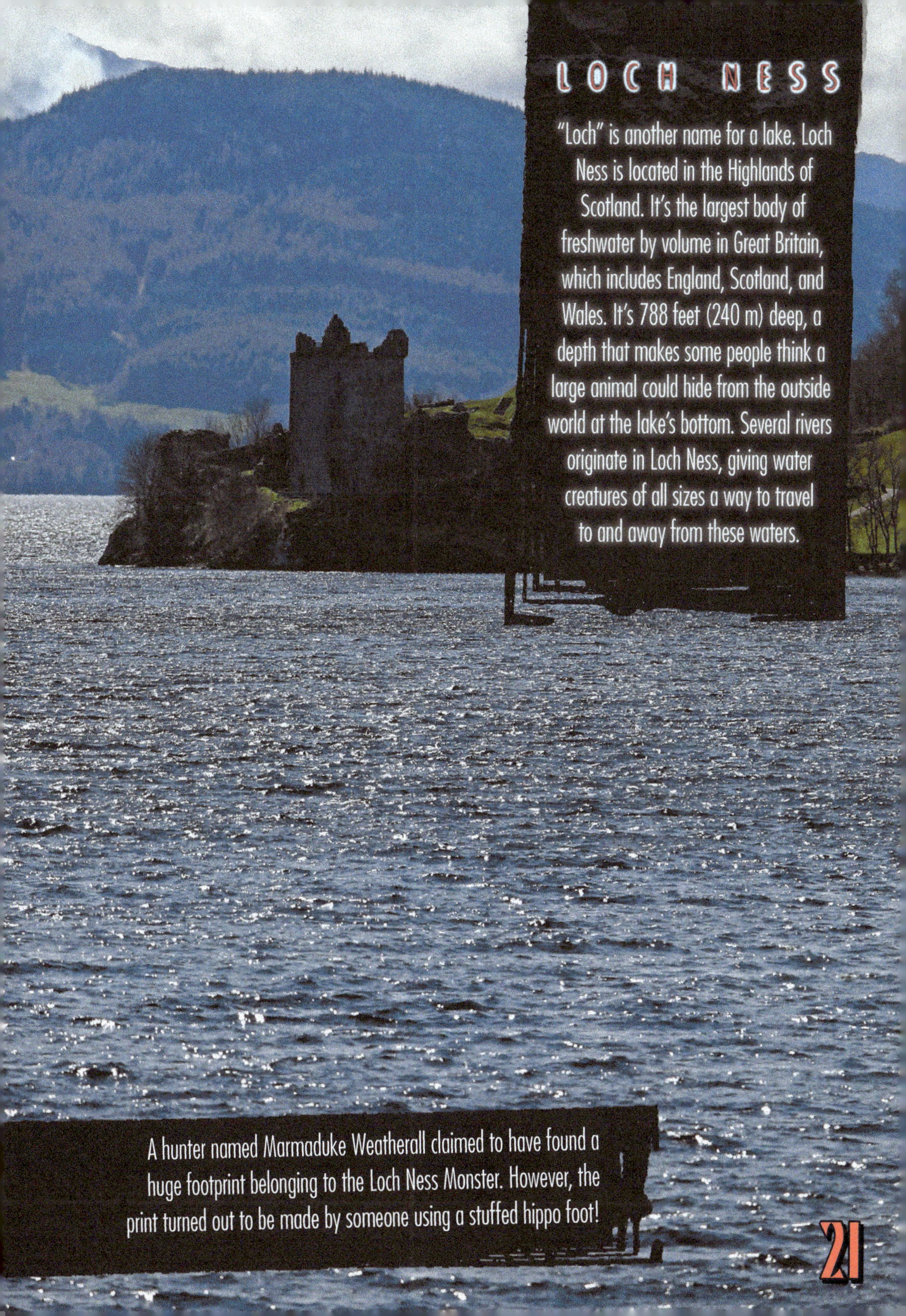

LOCH NESS

"Loch" is another name for a lake. Loch Ness is located in the Highlands of Scotland. It's the largest body of freshwater by volume in Great Britain, which includes England, Scotland, and Wales. It's 788 feet (240 m) deep, a depth that makes some people think a large animal could hide from the outside world at the lake's bottom. Several rivers originate in Loch Ness, giving water creatures of all sizes a way to travel to and away from these waters.

A hunter named Marmaduke Weatherall claimed to have found a huge footprint belonging to the Loch Ness Monster. However, the print turned out to be made by someone using a stuffed hippo foot!

REVEALED!

There have been reports of creatures similar to the Loch Ness Monster in lakes in Scandinavia.

People really began to wonder about a Loch Ness creature, or "Nessie" as the creature is sometimes called, when Scottish doctor R. Kenneth Wilson produced a photograph of a strange creature in 1934. Decades later, some people revealed the photo to be a fake, a trick played on a newspaper. One man claiming to have been involved said a fake head was placed on a toy submarine to make the "creature." However, the man who discovered the photo was a fake is a believer in the monster. He said he saw it himself!

As many as 4,000 visitors claimed to have seen the creature over the years, according to one author. Many are respected people who have no reason to lie about what they saw. So, what do you believe?

a 1969 submarine search for Nessie

SCIENCE SEARCHES FOR NESSIE

Scientific expeditions in Loch Ness have used underwater cameras and **sonar** to search the waters. Sonar has picked up large moving creatures, one even the size of a whale, but it's impossible to confirm what it was. A photograph revealed an animal with a large flipper, making one scientist believe it was a plesiosaur, a reptile thought to have died out with the dinosaurs. Could this creature have outlasted the dinosaurs by hiding in the depths of the loch?

This is the photo said to have been taken by the Scottish doctor in 1934. The Loch Ness Monster has also been seen crossing roads!

PREHISTORIC MONSTERS

Even if you don't think the Loch Ness Monster exists, without a doubt there were creatures much like it millions of years ago. From about 245 million years ago to about 66 million years ago, dinosaurs roamed Earth. Though some were plant eaters, others—such as *Tyrannosaurus rex*—were fierce predators who used powerful jaws to pull the flesh off their prey. The lesser-known *Spinosaurus* was truly a real-life monster. It was the largest predator ever on land!

Other animals back then were also scary compared to the animals we're accustomed to. The 30-foot (9 m) *Dunkleosteus* was a meat-eating fish with bony plates for teeth. The ancient snake *Titanoboa* was about 50 feet (15 m) long and weighed up to 2,500 pounds (1,135 kg)!

REVEALED!

Gigantopithecus **was a huge ape thought to have died out 100,000 years ago. Some think sightings of Bigfoot today may be a** ***Gigantopithecus*****!**

MEGALADON!

To many people, the most frightening animal they might encounter is a shark. The megaladon is the scariest shark to ever swim Earth's waters. It had a maximum length of 67 feet (20 m). That's more than three times the length of a great white shark. Scientists think its favorite prey were whales. Luckily for us, the megaladon died out about 1.5 million years ago.

Check out the spines on this *Spinosaurus*, one of the largest carnivores ever on Earth!

MONSTERS AMONG US

In September 2011, the people of the Bunawan township in the Philippines caught a very, very large crocodile. It was 21 feet (6.4 m) long and weighed 2,370 pounds (1,076 kg). Guinness World Records named it the largest crocodile in captivity.

The crocodile wasn't caught by accident. Twenty steel traps using animal carcasses as bait were set for it after at least one person went missing. It took almost 100 people to get the crocodile out of the water after it was caught! A wildlife official then made the crocodile throw up, but there was no proof it had eaten a human. There are thought to be about 1,000 other large crocodiles in that region of the Philippines. It might not have been the killer croc they were looking for!

REVEALED!

It took 3 weeks to capture the enormous crocodile in the Philippines. The crocodile, which was nicknamed "Lolong," was taken to a park where it was kept in a cage and cared for.

MOST DEADLY ANIMAL?

The most deadly animal in the world is the mosquito. Are you surprised? It's called the deadliest because it spreads a disease called malaria. The mosquito spreads the disease by sucking the blood of someone with malaria and then passing malaria to the next person it feeds on. Malaria is deadly if it's not treated. While it's not a problem in North America anymore, more than 620,000 people die of malaria each year, mostly in Africa.

Lolong died in captivity in 2013. He was thought to be about 50 years old.

Giant squid can grow to be 43 feet (13 m) long. With eight long arms and two **tentacles**, some people think it's possible that sea monster stories from years ago may really be about giant squid attacking ships.

People who are frightened of spiders fear the hairy tarantula. The largest, found in South America, can grow to be about 12 inches (30 cm) across and sometimes eats birds! Those who fear snakes might see green anacondas in their nightmares. The snakes reportedly reach 33 feet (10 m) long.

What kinds of monster animals do you fear? Are they as scary as Dracula, a werewolf, or Bigfoot? Whether they're real or make-believe, monsters of all shapes and sizes are fun to read about.

REVEALED!

The vampire bat does feed on blood, which is scary, but mostly the blood of cattle and horses.

green anaconda

WHAT ABOUT ZOMBIES?

Zombies as we know them in books and movies—undead people who roam trying to eat and infect the living—are somewhat new to popular culture. In lore, there are stories of walking dead, who are usually controlled by magic. In real life, there are zombie animals, animals infected by parasites that can control their behavior. For example, a kind of fungus can make a carpenter ant leave its colony and go to a place where the fungus can infect other ants.

tarantula

vampire bat

Do you think there are scarier animals out there that we don't know about?

GLOSSARY

abominable: very unpleasant or monstrous

afterlife: an existence after death

lore: traditional belief that has been handed down by word of mouth and usually told as stories

Mesopotamian: having to do with the ancient region located between the Tigris and the Euphrates Rivers in modern Iraq and Syria

peat bog: an area of marshy ground consisting of rotting plant matter

psychiatric: relating to a medical specialty concerned with disorders that have mental and behavioral symptoms

rabies: a potentially deadly disease that affects the central nervous system. It's carried in the spit of some animals.

sonar: a machine that uses sound waves to find things in a body of water

syringe: a tool that uses a hollow needle or tube to withdraw or inject fluids

tentacle: a long, thin body part that sticks out from an animal's head or mouth

tuberculosis: a sometimes deadly disease caused by a bacterium that especially affects the lungs

FOR MORE INFORMATION

BOOKS

Carney, Elizabeth. *Mummies*. Washington, DC: National Geographic, 2009.

Regan, Sally. *The Vampire Book: The Legends, the Lore, the Allure*. New York, NY: Dorling Kindersley Limited, 2009.

Schach, David. *The Loch Ness Monster*. Minneapolis, MN: Bellwether Media, 2011.

WEBSITES

15 Terrifying and Little Known Prehistoric Monsters
listverse.com/2010/03/30/15-terrifying-and-little-known-prehistoric-monsters/
Read and see illustrations of some scary real-life prehistoric creatures.

The Tollund Man
www.tollundman.dk
Read more about the mummified Tollund Man and what we know about the time and place in which he lived.

Publisher's note to educators and parents: Our editors have carefully reviewed these websites to ensure that they are suitable for students. Many websites change frequently, however, and we cannot guarantee that a site's future contents will continue to meet our high standards of quality and educational value. Be advised that students should be closely supervised whenever they access the Internet.

INDEX